Oceans

Joi Washington

 You can find sand in the ocean.

You can find shells in the ocean.  3

4 You can find rocks in the ocean.

You can find grass in the ocean.  5

 You can find crabs in the ocean.

You can find fish in the ocean.

 8 You can find octopuses in the ocean.

You can find turtles in the ocean.  9

 10 You can find jellyfish in the ocean.

You can find seahorses in the ocean.

 12 You can find penguins in the ocean.

You can find seals in the ocean.  13

 14 You can find dolphins in the ocean.

You can find whales in the ocean.  15

 16 You can find sharks in the ocean.

You can find people in the ocean.

Ocean Levels

surface

under water

ocean floor

18

Ocean Food Web

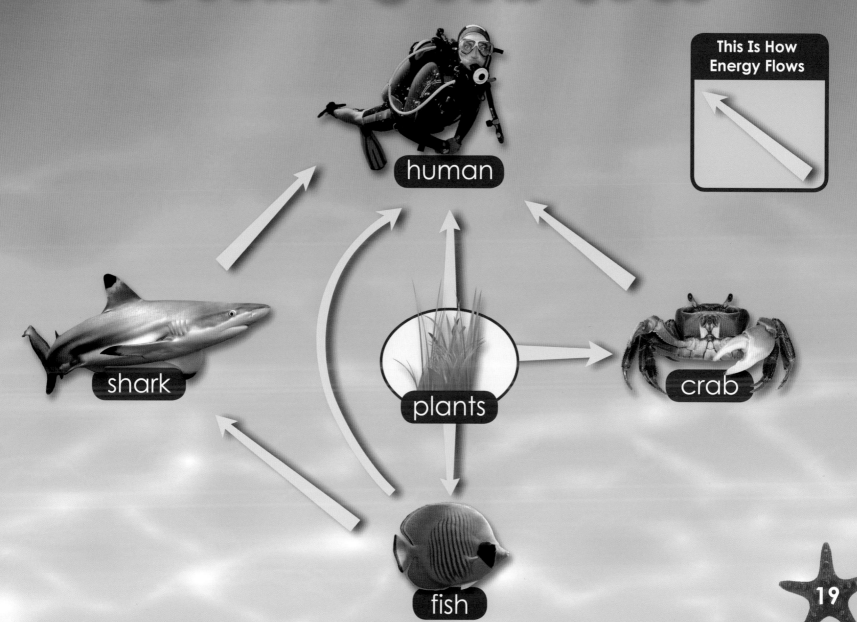

This Is How Energy Flows

human

shark

plants

crab

fish

19

Power Words

How many can you read?

You

you

can

in

the

20